M A R S

and the
Search
for
Life

ELAINE SCOTT

Clarion Books • New York

To Kathy and Bill Phares, Alice and George Watts—
the best siblings in the solar system!
With love, E.S.

ACKNOWLEDGMENTS

I am indebted to Antoinette Beiser, Librarian at the Lowell Observatory; Joy Demark for technical help with some of the images; Dr. Patricia Reiff at Rice University for heading the Rice Space Institute and inviting me to be part of it, and for putting me in the path of Steve Squyres, whose enthusiasm for the project is contagious and whose clarity on complicated topics is astonishing. I also want to thank Christine Shupla, Education Specialist, Lunar and Planetary Institute, for her expert reading of the text, and of course, everyone at Clarion Books: my editor, Jennifer Greene, for shaping the manuscript; managing editor Jim Armstrong, for correcting my mistakes; creative director Joann Hill, for consistently turning out beautiful books; and Trish Parcell Watts, for designing this one. All of you, along with everyone who worked on the MER mission, embody the spirit of the following quotation, largely attributed to Ralph Waldo Emerson: *"Do not go where the path may lead, go instead where there is no path and leave a trail."*

Clarion Books
an imprint of Houghton Mifflin Harcourt Publishing Company
215 Park Avenue South, New York, NY 10003
Copyright © 2008 by Elaine Scott
Book design by Trish Parcell Watts
The text was set in 14-point Berkeley.

www.clarionbooks.com

Manufactured in China

LIBRARY OF CONGRESS CATALOGING-IN-PUBLICATION DATA

Scott, Elaine, 1940–
Mars and the search for life / by Elaine Scott.
p. cm.
Includes bibliographical references and index.
ISBN 978-0-618-76695-6
1. Mars (Planet)—Juvenile literature. 2. Life on other planets—Juvenile literature.
I. Title.
QB54.S365 2008
576.8'39099923—dc22
2008007243

WKT 10 9 8 7 6 5 4 3 2 1

Please note that some of the images provided by NASA throughout the book are composites based on technical drawings, photographs, or other scientific data, and that NASA does not credit the individual artists, scientists, or engineers who create them. All such images are identified in their captions as "artist's conception."

The image of Mars that appears opposite as well as the images on pages 52, 55, 57, 59 are parts of a composite of 100 Viking Orbiter images taken in 1980. The full composite appears on page 26.

CONTENTS

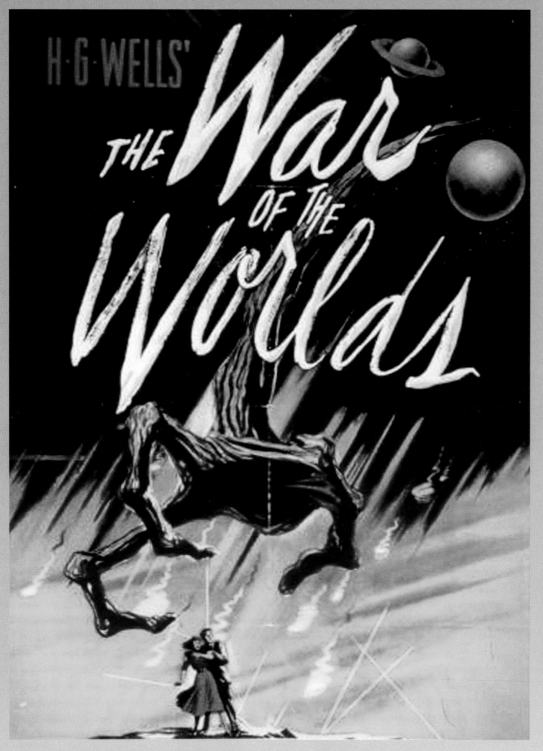

A poster from Paramount Pictures' 1953 film version of *The War of the Worlds.*
Getty Images/Hulton Archive

An illustration from the 1906 edition of the book.
Mary Evans Picture Library/Alamy

Tom Cruise starred in Steven Spielberg's 2005 version. *Alamy*

INTRODUCTION

It was October 30, 1938—the day before Halloween. In some parts of the United States they called it "Mischief Night," a time when children felt free to play tricks on their friends. However, by 8:00 P.M., most children were home, dinner was over, and families were settling in for an evening of listening to their favorite radio programs. *Mercury Theatre on the Air* was very popular with adults. It featured plays directed by, and often starring, a young actor named Orson Welles.

The show began, and after it had been under way for a while, an announcer broke in declaring, "At twenty minutes before eight, Central time, Professor Farrell of the Mount Jennings Observatory, Chicago, Illinois, reports observing several explosions of incandescent gas, occurring at regular intervals on the planet Mars." The announcer went on to say the gas was moving toward Earth "with enormous velocity." But there was no panic. Not yet.

Then, in another interruption a few minutes later, he proclaimed that a "huge flaming object" had dropped onto a farmer's field near Grovers Mill, New Jersey. This was followed by an anxious report, as the "object" opened.

Since its publication in 1898, H. G. Wells's novel *The War of the Worlds* has been adapted dozens of times for movies, radio scripts, and video games, and as a graphic novel.

A reporter on the scene provided details. "Good heavens, something's wriggling out of the shadow like a gray snake. Now it's another one, and another one, and another one! . . . It's large, large as a bear and it glistens like wet leather. But that face, it . . . Ladies and gentlemen, it's indescribable."

The reporter described it anyway. "The eyes are black and gleam like a serpent. The mouth is V-shaped, with saliva dripping from its rimless lips that seem to quiver and pulsate. The monster or whatever it is can hardly move. It seems weighed down by . . . possibly gravity or something."

And then came this statement: "Incredible as it may seem, both the observations of science and the evidence of our eyes lead to the inescapable assumption that those strange beings who landed in the Jersey farmlands tonight are the vanguard of an invading army from the planet Mars."

These vivid descriptions were accompanied by appropriate sound effects, as the "strange beings" hissed, gas escaped, and witnesses screamed in terror.

Before long, real terror spread among those who were listening to the broadcast. Many abandoned their radio sets and fled into the streets with wet towels over their heads, hoping to protect themselves from the poisonous Martian gas. Others hid in their basements in an attempt to avoid the coming disaster. Police and fire station telephones rang continuously, as callers begged for information on how the authorities were going to protect them from the Martians.

The following day, the *New York Times* ran a story headlined "Radio Listeners in Panic, Taking War Drama as Fact." The opening paragraph of the article reported, "A wave of mass hysteria seized thousands of radio listeners . . . last night when a broadcast of a dramatization of H. G. Wells's fantasy, 'The War of the Worlds,' led thousands to believe that an inter-

Orson Welles broadcasting "The War of the Worlds" for *Mercury Theatre on the Air*. Bettmann/Corbis

planetary conflict had started with invading Martians spreading wide death and destruction in New Jersey and New York."

Few listeners, it seems, had paid attention to the opening words of the broadcast, which were, "The Columbia Broadcasting System and its affiliated stations present Orson Welles and the Mercury Theatre on the Air in 'The War of the Worlds' by H. G. Wells." Nor did they pay attention to another announcement at the end of the show, when Mr. Welles said, "This is Orson Welles, ladies and gentlemen, out of character to assure you that 'The War of the Worlds' has no further significance than as the holiday offering it was intended to be . . . [a] radio version of dressing up in a sheet and jumping out of a bush and saying Boo!"

It was Mischief Night, and it was only a story—a radio play based on English author Wells's 1898 science fiction novel about an imagined Martian invasion of Earth. Yet despite the statements at the beginning and the end of the show, thousands of people believed the invasion was really happening.

Why? Perhaps because in their hearts the audience *wanted* to believe there is life on other planets. That kind of thinking is not unusual. From the beginning of time, people have gazed up into a night sky full of stars and planets and wondered, *Are we alone?*

From ancient myths to comic books, stories about Mars have always been popular.
Mary Evans Picture Library/Alamy

1. OBSERVING MARS

From the beginning of history, Mars, the small red planet that is fourth from the Sun, has always fascinated—even frightened—those who have watched it move from east to west across the night sky. Ages ago, people may have looked at Mars's reddish color and thought of all the blood that is spilled during war. Perhaps that is why the ancient Assyrians called Mars the "Shedder of Blood," and the Greeks, Romans, and, later, the Vikings named the planet after their gods of war. Mars was ancient Rome's god of war, and that is the name that has endured.

Our earliest ancestors used stories and myths to explain the mysteries of nature. They knew little about science, as we think of it today. Nevertheless, astronomy, the study of the universe beyond Earth, is one of the world's oldest sciences. The earliest astronomers, like Ptolemy (TOLE-uh-me) (approximately A.D 100–179), who lived in Roman Egypt, didn't have telescopes or other instruments to help them study the moon and the stars. They had to rely on their own eyesight. Then, in 1608, the telescope was invented by a Dutch optician, Hans Lippershey (LIP-er-shy), who lived from 1570 to 1619.

Two natural wonders in the night sky: Mars shares the sky with the bands of light known as the aurora borealis, or northern lights. Car headlights and taillights appear as red and white streaks at the bottom of this time-lapse photograph. *Fotosearch*

Lippershey's invention had two lenses at either end of a tube. One, called a convex lens, curved outward. It made objects appear bigger than they were, but blurry. The smaller lens, called a concave lens, curved inward. It made objects look smaller, but clearer. When light passed through both lenses, objects appeared three to four times larger and closer than they were. Just a year later, in 1609, the Italian Galileo Galilei (ga-luh-LAY-oh ga-luh-LAY-ee) (1564–1642) made improvements to the instrument that enabled it to make objects appear 20 times larger than their true size.

Telescopes continued to improve. Galileo's was five to six feet in length, but by the middle of the 17th century, telescopes had grown. In 1656, a telescope made by Dutch mathematician Christiaan Huygens (HOY-gehns) (1629–1695) was 23 feet long and could magnify 100 times.

The telescope changed astronomy forever. Knowledge of the universe grew, and ancient ideas gave way to new ones. The belief that Earth was at the center of our solar system gave way to the theory that the Sun was at the center.

Astronomers continued to observe the planets and stars and make notes about what they saw. In 1877, an Italian astronomer, Giovanni Schiaparelli (joh-VON-ne skyah-puh-REL-lee) (1835–1910) trained his telescope on Mars and made a surprising discovery. He announced that the planet seemed to be crisscrossed by a series of channels—or, in Italian, *canali*. Unfortunately, when Schiaparelli's work was translated into English, a mistake was made. The word *canali* was translated as the word "canals." Though both are waterways, a canal is built by people, while a channel is created by nature. Debate raged among the astronomers of the day: Had the waterways on Mars been created by intelligent beings, or were they natural Martian formations? Throughout his life, Schiaparelli

An engraving showing Hans Lippershey's apprentices looking through two lenses at once. *Mary Evans Picture Library/Alamy*

Refracting vs. Reflecting

There are two major types of telescope—refractors and reflectors. *Refracting* telescopes, like the ones used by Lippershey and Galileo, have lenses that refract, or bend, the light that passes through them. Light enters the telescope and passes through the larger convex lens at the front, then is bent toward the smaller concave lens at the back of the telescope. Because light is broken into the colors of the spectrum when it is bent, objects seen with the earliest telescopes had colors around their edges. Isaac Newton solved that problem in 1668 by constructing the first *reflecting* telescope. It used mirrors to reflect, rather than refract, the light from the objects it observed. Both refracting and reflecting telescopes, as well as combinations of the two, are used today.

remained neutral on the question. However, many of those who read Schiaparelli's papers in English believed they were reading about constructed canals, and they drew the conclusion that these canals had been made by a civilization living on Mars. The American astronomer Percival Lowell (1855–1916) was among the biggest believers.

In 1894, Percival Lowell established the Lowell Observatory on top of Mars Hill in Flagstaff, Arizona. For 23 years, Lowell worked at his observatory, studying Mars and making drawings of the features he saw through his telescope. As he observed Schiaparelli's "canals," he became convinced they had been built by intelligent beings. Lowell promoted his views in three books: *Mars*, published in 1895, *Mars and Its Canals* (1906), and *Mars as the Abode of Life* (1908). In *Mars*, Lowell wrote, "Certainly what we see hints at the existence of beings who are in advance of, not behind us, in the journey of life." Though we know now that he was incorrect, Percival

Italian astronomer Giovanni Schiaparelli mapped the surface of Mars in 1877. *The Lowell Observatory*

LEFT: Percival Lowell with the 24-inch telescope at the Lowell Observatory. He was convinced that intelligent life existed on Mars.
The Lowell Observatory

BELOW: Lowell's 1905 drawing of Mars, showing the "canals" he believed were there.

Lowell was relying upon scientific "evidence" to formulate a hypothesis, or prediction, about what Martian life might be like.

At the same time, another man, the English writer H. G. Wells (1866–1946), was using his imagination to form a very different picture of life on Mars. In 1898, Wells's science fiction novel *The War of the Worlds*—which was later used as the basis for the famous radio broadcast—was published. It was one of the first books to describe an alien invasion from another planet.

Thanks to the scientific efforts of Lowell and others, and the creative effort of H. G. Wells, the idea of a habitable world somewhere else in our solar system began to capture the world's imagination.

H. G. Wells at his writing desk. *Lebrecht Music and Arts Photo Library/Alamy*

More About Mars

An Earth-Mars comparison
NASA/Goddard Space Flight Center

- Mars is the fourth planet from the Sun.
- Mars orbits the Sun at an average distance of 141.5 million miles.
- Mars's distance from Earth varies, according to the orbits of both planets. At its closest, Mars is 33.9 million miles away. At its farthest, it is 249 million miles away.
- Mars is about half the size of Earth, though its land area is about the same. This is because our planet is covered with oceans, and Mars is not.
- Because it is smaller than Earth, Mars's gravity is only 38 percent as strong as Earth's. A human weighing 160 pounds on Earth would weigh only about 60 pounds on Mars.
- Mars has two tiny moons—Phobos and Deimos. Phobos means "fear," and Deimos means "panic." In mythology, Phobos and Deimos were the offspring of Mars. The moons were discovered in 1877 by Asaph Hall, working at the U.S. Naval Observatory.
- The month of March takes its name from Mars.
- One Martian day, or "sol," lasts 24 hours, 39 minutes, and 35 seconds.
- Traveling at an average speed of 53,979 mph, it takes Mars 687 Earth days to make one orbit around the Sun.
- Mars boasts both the largest volcano and the largest canyon system in the solar system.
- The average temperature on Mars is −64 degrees Fahrenheit, but at its poles the temperature can dip to −225°F and at the equator it can rise to 80°F.
- Martian wind can blow at hurricane force—more than 75 miles per hour.

*Source: NASA. Please note that statistics may vary slightly among sources.

2. WET OR DRY?

Percival Lowell was certain that Mars had water and that the "canals" he saw carried it from one place to another. H. G. Wells had a different idea. His story told the tale of a dry planet, with little water. In fact, in his novel the Martians invade Earth in a desperate search for water and other resources. The scientist and the novelist agreed on one thing, however: water is necessary for life. From a tiny microbe to a complex human being, no living thing can exist without liquid water.

Earth is a very wet planet. About 71 percent of its surface is covered by its seven oceans—the Arctic, the North Atlantic, the South Atlantic, the North Pacific, the South Pacific, the Indian, and the Southern. But even when using the most powerful ground-based telescopes on Earth, it was simply impossible to tell, just by looking, whether Mars had oceans or not. And then on October 4, 1957, things changed. Science took a leap into space.

On that date, the Soviet Union (today's Russia) launched the world's first artificial satellite, *Sputnik I*, into space. On July 29, 1958, the U.S. Congress responded by establishing the National Aeronautics and Space Administration (NASA).

Earth has abundant liquid water.
R. Stockli, A. Nelson, F. Hasler, NASA/GSFC/NOAA/USOS

NASA is the official U.S. government organization responsible for the human exploration of space. Over the next several years, the United States, the Soviet Union (the U.S.S.R.), and other countries sent spacecraft to explore the planets of our solar system. Information about Mars began to grow, but some of it was disappointing.

RIIGHT: The launch of *Sputnik* began the Space Age. The world's first artificial satellite weighed 183 pounds and orbited Earth every 98 minutes, sending back a beeping signal. *NASA/Asif A. Siddiq*

BELOW: The 1957 launch of *Sputnik* began the space race between the U.S.S.R. and the United States. By 1958 American schools had responded by adding more science to their curricula. These students in Hagerstown, Maryland, presented what they had learned in a program called "A Visit to the Planets."

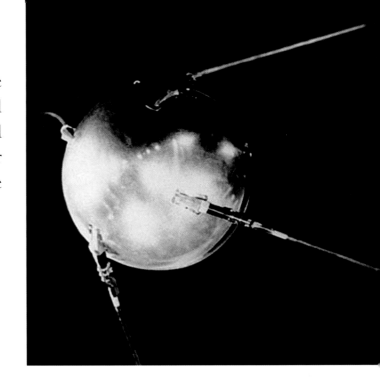

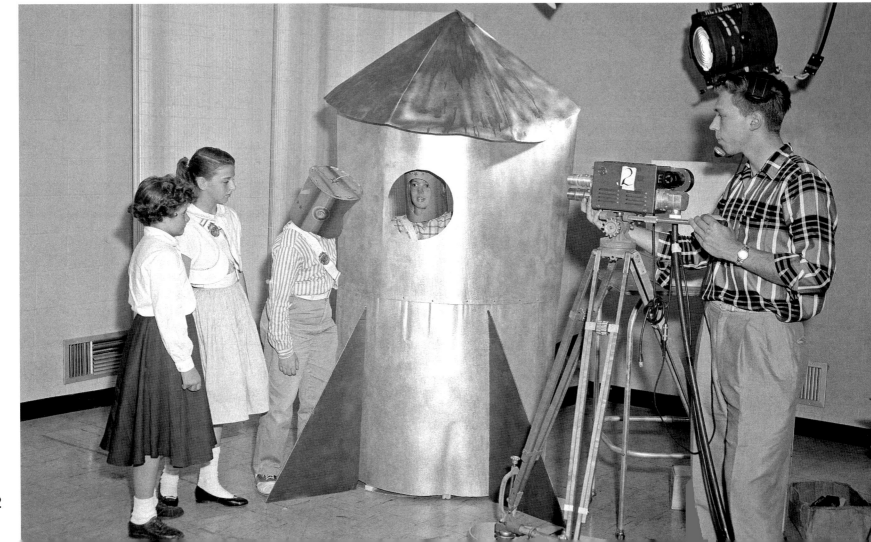

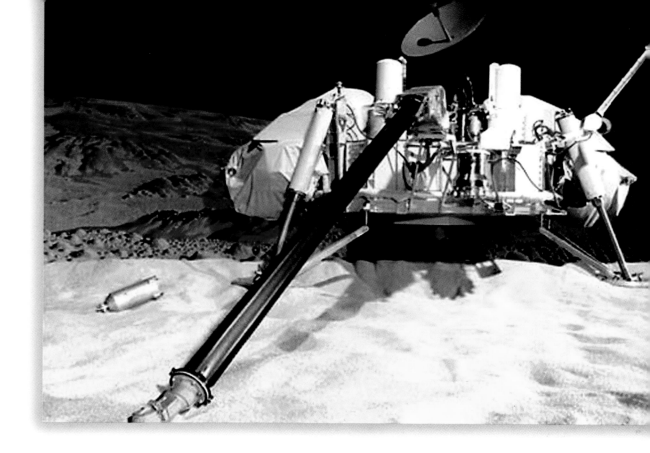

An artist's conception of the *Viking* lander that provided the first photographs ever taken from the surface of Mars. The *Viking* spacecraft were named after the Vikings, who were the first European explorers of North America. *NASA*

The first color image from *Viking* Lander 1. The *Viking* pictures caused a sensation and laid the groundwork for future missions to Mars. *NASA/JPL-Caltech*

In 1965, *Mariner 4* flew by Mars and sent back 21 images. They were the first close-up photographs ever taken of another planet. By 1969, *Mariner 6* and *Mariner 7* had returned images that proved that the canals Lowell thought were irrigation channels were either an optical illusion or perhaps streaks of wind-blown dust along crater floors. They were not any kind of irrigation ditch—natural or constructed. Mars appeared to be a dry, dead planet.

Then in 1976, two U.S. spacecraft, *Viking 1* and *Viking 2*, flew *to* Mars, instead of past it. In addition to orbiting the planet, these missions sent landers to Mars's surface. The *Viking* photographs that were returned to Earth revealed a far different planet than had been seen before. Mars was still a cold, lifeless place. It was still dry, with no sign of liquid water. There were still craters scattered about. But the pictures revealed some exciting new features, too. They showed that

Mars was a planet with two main regions—low plains in the north, and cratered hills, or highlands, in the south. Volcanoes dotted the landscape. One, Olympus Mons, was nearly three times as tall as Mt. Everest! These volcanoes had created plains of lava. The *Viking* pictures showed a canyon near Mars's equator, later named Valles Marineris, that was so wide and so long that it made Earth's Grand Canyon look like a crack in the sidewalk. And by 1976, scientists knew that the poles contained both water ice and ice in the form of frozen carbon dioxide, or "dry ice." In addition, the *Viking* photographs seemed to reveal features that looked like dry riverbeds, similar to the riverbeds carved by flowing water on Earth.

As they pored over the images, geologists (scientists who study the origin and history of Earth and other planets by examining rocks, soil, and other features) began to speculate. If Mars had once had rivers, it could have had oceans, too. And life could have formed in those oceans, as life first formed in the oceans of Earth. Still, the photographs showed that

TOP: Valles Marineris, taken from the *Mars Odyssey* orbiter. This canyon is six to seven times deeper than the Grand Canyon; if it were on Earth, it would stretch across the United States. *NASA/JPL-Arizona State University*

ABOVE: Olympus Mons volcano, taken from the *Viking* orbiter. Olympus Mons stands almost 15 miles high and over 300 miles wide. It is the largest volcano in our solar system. *NASA/JPL-Caltech*

liquid water, if it had ever been there, had now disappeared. So scientists had other questions. If there had once been water on Mars, what happened to make it disappear? Was Mars once warmer than it is now? If its climate had changed, what happened to cause the change—and could the same thing happen to Earth?

Scientists from around the world were eager to answer these questions. More missions to Mars were planned. Clearly, the planet still had information to reveal.

Missions to Mars

The Soviet Union made the first attempt to reach Mars in 1960. The mission failed to reach Earth orbit. As of early 2008, there have been 39 attempts to either orbit Mars or put a lander on its surface. Of those 39 attempts, only 14 were complete successes, two were partially successful, and as of this writing, one is still to be determined. The *Phoenix* lander launched on August 4, 2007, and landed safely on Mars on May 25, 2008, as this book went to press.

SUCCESSFUL MARS MISSIONS

Year	Name	Country	Result
1964	Mariner 4	U.S.	Returned 21 images.
1969	Mariner 6	U.S.	Returned 75 images.
1969	Mariner 7	U.S.	Returned 126 images.
1971	Mars 3 Orbiter/Lander	U.S.S.R.	Partial success. Orbiter obtained approximately 9 months of data. Lander arrived on surface safely but obtained only 20 seconds of data.
1971	Mariner 9	U.S.	Returned 7,329 images.
1973	Mars 5	U.S.S.R.	Returned 60 images; lasted 9 days.
1973	Mars 6	U.S.S.R.	Partial success. Cameras and instruments produced information, but lander failed on descent.
1975	Viking 1 Orbiter/Lander	U.S.	First successful landing on Mars.
1975	Viking 2 Orbiter/Lander	U.S.	Returned 16,000 images and extensive atmospheric data and performed soil experiments.
1996	Mars Global Surveyor	U.S.	Returned more images than all previous Mars missions.
1996	Mars Pathfinder	U.S.	First U.S. mission to send lander with rover to Mars. Sent images back indicating Mars was possibly once warm and wet. Last transmission on September 27, 1997.
2001	Mars Odyssey	U.S.	Odyssey images helped plot landing sites for Mars rovers *Spirit* and *Opportunity.* Also serves as a communication link between the rovers and Earth.
2003	Mars Express Orbiter/Beagle 2 Lander	ESA	European Space Agency. Partial success. Mars Express Orbiter still returning photos of Mars's surface. Beagle 2 lander was lost on arrival.
2003	Mars Exploration Rover—Spirit	U.S.	Currently providing surface information on Mars's geology, atmosphere, and conditions that could support past or present microbial life, including the presence of water. Mission extended to 2009.
2003	Mars Exploration Rover—Opportunity	U.S.	Currently providing surface information on Mars's geology, atmosphere, and conditions that could support past or present microbial life, including presence of water. Mission extended to 2009.
2005	Mars Reconnaissance Orbiter	U.S.	Returned more images than all previous Mars's missions combined, including close-up photography of Mars's surface. Mission scheduled to end December 31, 2010, but could be extended.
2007	Phoenix Mars Lander	U.S.	Successfully landed on Mars May 25, 2008; success of remainder of mission to be determined.

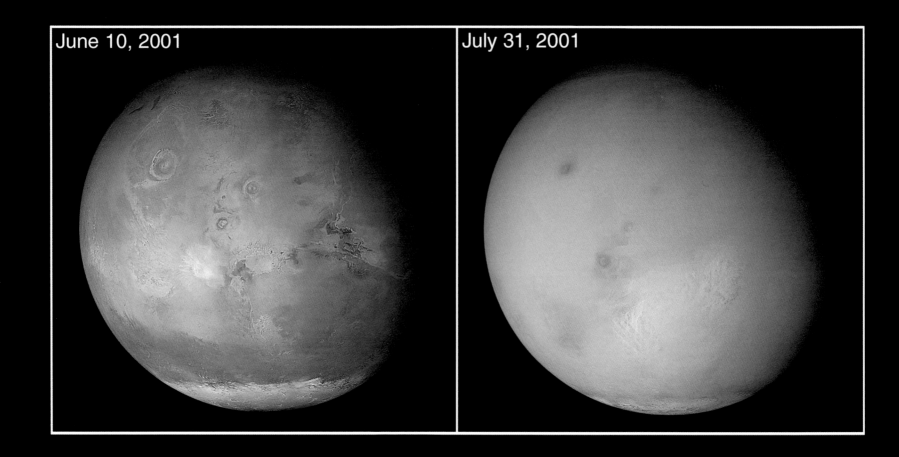

3. PROPOSALS AND PAYLOADS

The first U.S. missions to Mars were flybys. As the word implies, the spacecraft simply flew to Mars and took pictures as they passed by the planet. *Mariners* 3 and 4 in 1964 and *Mariners* 6 and 7 in 1969 were flyby missions. Next came *Viking 1* and *Viking 2*, which entered Mars's orbit and sent landers to its surface. And then there was a long period of time—20 years—when the United States did not have a successful mission to Mars. That dry spell was broken on November 7, 1996, with the successful launch of the *Mars Global Surveyor* (MGS).

The *MGS* was a mapping mission designed to examine the entire planet from orbit. Its first radio transmission to Earth came on September 12, 1997. In the years following that first transmission, the scientific instruments onboard the *MGS* have sent valuable information to scientists searching for signs of life. The *MGS* revealed that Mars has seasons that repeat in a pattern. Dust storms come and go at approximately the same time, in the same location, year after year. And photos from the *MGS* showed gullies that seemed to indicate that water had once been on Mars, either on the surface or right below it,

On June 10, 2001, Mars was free of dust storms. However, by late June, several large storms began to form, and by July 31, the planet was covered in dust.
NASA/JPL/Malin Space Science Systems

though later studies concluded it was more likely that the gullies were formed by avalanches of dust and rock. Knowing when dust storms are likely to occur, and knowing where water might have once flowed, was invaluable as NASA prepared for future missions to Mars. The *MGS* last communicated with scientists on Earth on November 2, 2006. NASA believes the satellite then lost its battery power.

A month after the *MGS* was launched, another mission, called *Mars Pathfinder*, headed to the red planet. It carried the first robotic explorer, the rover *Sojourner*, to Mars. Part of the mission's objective was to demonstrate that rovers were capable

The tiny rover *Sojourner* was the first robotic rover on Mars. It was named for Sojourner Truth, a former slave who became an advocate for civil rights. *NASA/JPL*

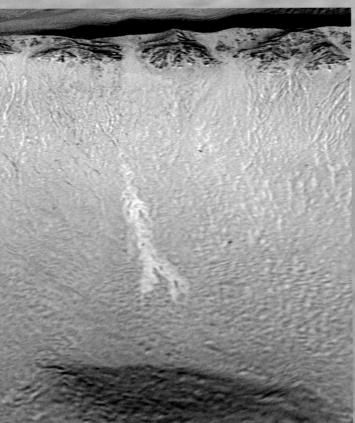

of exploring Mars's surface. The results from the 83 days *Sojourner* worked on Mars were exciting. At a press conference held on October 8, 1997, at the end of the mission, project scientist Dr. Matthew Golumbek said, "What the data are telling us is that the planet appears to have water-worn rock conglomerates, sand and surface features that were created by liquid water." He added, "Water, of course, is the very ingredient that is necessary to support life, and that leads to the $64,000 question: Are we alone in the universe? Did life ever develop on Mars? If so, what happened to it and, if not, why not?"

A few months earlier, on June 7, 1997, NASA had issued an Announcement of Opportunity (AO). Engineers at NASA's Jet Propulsion Laboratory (JPL) in California announced a new mission, the *Mars Exploration Rover* mission, or *MER*. The goal was to learn more about the history of water on the planet. The engineers at JPL would create two robotic rovers that would examine the rocks on Mars, looking for signs that they may have formed in water. Scientists from around the world were invited to compete to put their instruments onboard these rovers.

In order to be considered for this mission, every scientific team had to write a proposal that described the kinds of instruments they would design, what those instruments would do on Mars, and how much it would cost to build them. It is expensive to send anything into space, and the cargo, the most important part of the mission, is appropriately called the "payload." If the mission is a scientific one, then the payload is

TOP: An artist's conception of the *Mars Global Surveyor. NASA/JPL*

BOTTOM: At first, scientists believed these gullies, photographed by the *MGS*, were formed by liquid water, but new evidence suggests they were more likely formed by an avalanche of soil. *NASA/JPL/Malin Space Science Systems*

made up of the equipment that is necessary to conduct the experiments. On the other hand, if the mission is one to repair something in space—such as a space telescope or part of the International Space Station—then the payload becomes the tools and equipment necessary to accomplish that task.

The *MER* payload would consist of scientific instruments and the two rovers. Many scientists from around the world responded to the AO with excitement. There was a lot of competition to create the payload for this mission.

Dr. Steven Squyres is a professor of astronomy at Cornell University in Ithaca, New York, and for years he and a team of other scientists from the university had been working toward the goal of sending scientific instruments to Mars. Their project had a name, Athena, for the Greek goddess of wisdom, and their goal was to have the Athena project be chosen as the payload for the *MER* mission.

On November 7, 1997, NASA selected the proposal Steve Squyres and his team had submitted. Steve was named the project's principal scientific investigator. In a way, because their instruments were going to Mars, it was almost as if the entire Athena team was going there, too.

Steve Squyres, Ph.D., is the Goldwin Smith Professor of Astronomy at Cornell University. He was the lead scientist on the NASA *Mars Exploration Rover* mission.
Wenski-Roberts/Cornell University

4. SPIRIT AND OPPORTUNITY

Sofi Collis was born in Siberia and later adopted and brought to the United States. When she was nine, she entered an essay-writing contest to name the rovers, and her entry won. Here is part of what she wrote: "I used to live in an orphanage. It was dark and cold and lonely. At night, I looked up at the sparkly sky and felt better. I dreamed I could fly there. In America, I can make all my dreams come true. Thank you for the 'Spirit' and the 'Opportunity.'" And so the rovers got their names—*Spirit* and *Opportunity*.

On a project like *MER*, scientists and engineers have to cooperate with each other, because each discipline's goals are slightly different. The scientists want to send all their instruments to Mars. The engineers want to design and build a spacecraft that can safely land on Mars. Just as you can't stuff too many clothes into a suitcase without wrinkling them or straining the suitcase, you can't stuff too many scientific instruments aboard a spacecraft, either. The Athena team from Cornell worked carefully with the engineering team at JPL to make certain their instruments would fit inside the rovers. And

Sofi Collis was in third grade when NASA Administrator Sean O'Keefe announced that her entry had been chosen from among 10,000 in the contest to name the rovers. Here she is shown at the awards ceremony at the Kennedy Space Center in June 2003.
NASA/JPL/Kennedy Space Center

the JPL engineers worked to design a spacecraft that would transport the rovers to Mars and land them safely on the planet's surface.

Steve Squyres described the work the identical golf cart–sized rovers would do on Mars. "Think of *Spirit* and *Opportunity* as robotic field geologists. They go to the rocks that seem most interesting. When they get to one, they reach out with a robotic arm that has a handful of tools, a microscope, two instruments for identifying what the rock is made of, and a grinder for getting to a fresh, unweathered surface inside the rock." All of the rovers' tools were going to be used to "read" the rocks on Mars.

Every rock is made up of building blocks known as minerals. When minerals are studied in a certain way, their composition reveals how they came to be part of that particular rock. On Earth, geologists know that some minerals are formed only under water. Other minerals are altered when hot water runs through them. By "reading the rocks," or determining their

A Tool with a Tribute

There is something special about grinders on the rovers. The Rock Abrasion Tools—or RATS, for short—were designed by a company called Honeybee Robotics, which has its headquarters in Lower Manhattan, close to the site of the Twin Towers of the World Trade Center. When the towers were attacked and destroyed on September 11, 2001, the employees at Honeybee were devastated. Everyone wanted to do something to honor those who had lost their lives. Steve Kondos, an engineer at the Jet Propulsion Laboratory who was working with Honeybee's RAT team, came up with the idea of incorporating some of the wreckage from the Twin Towers into the mission to Mars. With the permission of the mayor's office, parts of the twisted aluminum from both Towers were delivered to Honeybee Robotics. There, the pieces were hammered until they were straight. Then they were sent to another company where they were polished and molded into protective sleeves for the cables on the RATs. Next, an American flag, in the form of a special decal that could resist Mars's harsh climate, was placed on each sleeve. Now each rover would carry two important symbols of the United States to Mars.

The RAT at work. *NASA/JPL-Caltech*

An artist's conception of a Mars rover. *Spirit* and *Opportunity* are identical robots. *NASA/JPL*

mineral composition, geologists can tell whether they formed in water or on dry land, and they can tell whether a rock had once been dry but then was altered by water running through—or over—it. The rocks and soil on Earth will always reveal their history. The rocks and soil of Mars will do the same thing—provided a good geologist gets a chance to study them. Since no human geologist could go to Mars, the robotic rovers would have to do the work. The information they gathered would then be studied by scientists here on Earth.

Instruments Onboard the Rovers

There are seven primary scientific instruments onboard each rover.

Panoramic Camera (Pancam). The Pancam acts as the rover's "eyes." It is mounted on a five-foot mast and provides a 360-degree, humanlike view of the Martian terrain.

Miniature Thermal Emission Spectrometer (Mini-TES). A spectrometer is an optical instrument that measures the amount of heat coming from an object. Different substances emit heat differently, and scientists can study the heat patterns to determine what kind of minerals are in the various rocks and soils on Mars. Mini-TES is located at the bottom of the rover's mast, where it is protected from the harsh Martian climate, while the mast acts as a kind of periscope. Mirrors at the top of the mast collect the infrared heat, or light, from the object that is being studied and send it down to the Mini-TES for analysis. The mirrors in the mast can also be pointed to the Martian sky to take the atmospheric temperature and provide information about the climate.

Magnets. Magnets are used to collect magnetic dust particles. Those particles are then analyzed by the Mössbauer Spectrometer and the Alpha Particle X-Ray Spectrometer.

Mössbauer Spectrometer (MB). This instrument can identify substances that contain iron by placing its sensor, mounted on a robotic "arm," against the Martian soil. The rocks and soil of Mars are rich in iron.

Alpha Particle X-Ray Spectrometer (APXS). This is a microscopic instrument that can determine how much silicon, how much magnesium, how much iron or other elements, a particular rock contains.

Microscopic Imager (MI). The MI is a combination microscope and camera designed to take clear, close-up photographs of the rocks and soil on Mars.

Rock Abrasion Tool (RAT). The RAT is a combination of grinder and brush that removes dusty and weathered rock surfaces to reveal fresh material that can then be examined by the other instruments.

The information gathered by these instruments is sent via radio signal to the *Mars Odyssey* satellite orbiting above the planet, and from there to Mission Control at the Jet Propulsion Laboratory in California.

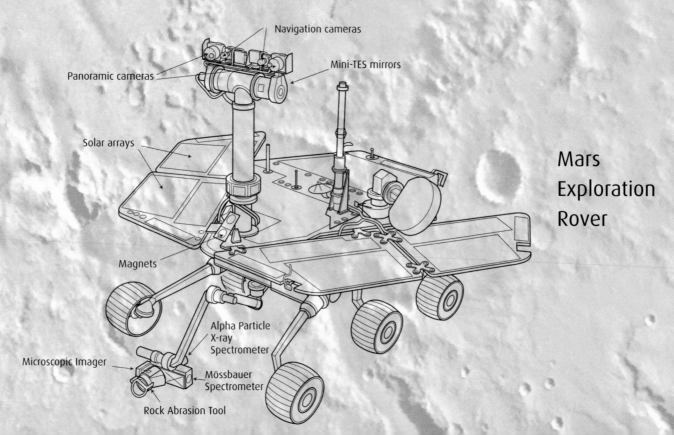

Navigation cameras

Panoramic cameras

Mini-TES mirrors

Solar arrays

Magnets

Mars Exploration Rover

Microscopic Imager

Alpha Particle X-ray Spectrometer

Mössbauer Spectrometer

Rock Abrasion Tool

In addition to the scientific instruments, the rovers had solar arrays to gather energy from the Sun. And because Mars is a very dusty planet, the rovers carried special magnets to collect the dust and analyze it. *Spirit* and *Opportunity* were also equipped with cameras to photograph the Martian rocks and terrain. Additional navigation cameras onboard enabled the rovers to "see" where they were going. And where they were going was Gusev Crater and Meridiani Planum.

5. GUSEV CRATER AND MERIDIANI PLANUM

After NASA scientists spent more than two years studying more than 150 other possibilities, the decision was made to send *Spirit* to Gusev Crater, and *Opportunity* to Meridiani Planum. The selection committee had a lot to consider, including safety and science. No one wanted to have the rovers land at a place that was too rugged or too rocky, or had too many dust storms. Landing on a jagged rock could damage the rovers' wheels immediately; rugged terrain could damage the rovers as soon as they started to move. And if too much dust settled on the rovers' solar arrays, it could prevent them from collecting energy from the Sun—energy they would need to charge their batteries and operate.

For that same reason, it was important that the rovers work near Mars's equator. As on Earth, because of the tilt of the planet on its axis, daylight and dark on Mars are most evenly divided all year long at the equator. The maximum and most consistent amount of daylight made the equator the place where the rovers' batteries would get the most power.

Gusev Crater and Meridiani Planum were safe places to land; they were near the equator; and most important of all,

Destination: Mars. This image is a composite of 100 *Viking* orbiter images, taken in 1980. *NASA/JPL*

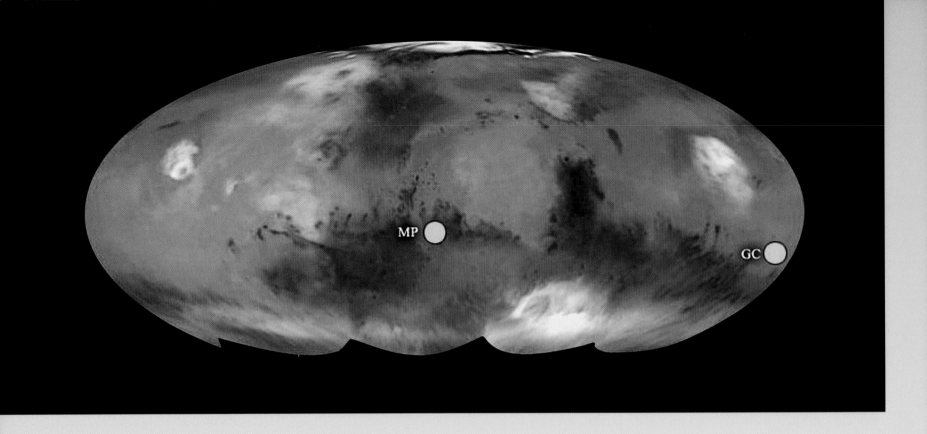

A flattened view of Mars, showing the two landing sites, Meridiani Planum and Gusev Crater—on opposite sides of the planet. *NASA/JPL-Caltech*

photographs taken by the three satellites orbiting Mars at the time suggested that liquid water had once been present at both locations.

Scientists believe that an asteroid, or a comet, may have hit Mars three to four *billion* years ago and that the impact formed Gusev Crater, which is about the size of the state of Connecticut. The base of the crater is about 95 miles across, and is pockmarked with other, newer craters created by more recent impacts. Photographs from the orbiting satellites seemed to indicate that a channel of some kind once opened into Gusev, and scientists have hypothesized that billions of years ago the channel carried water into Gusev, creating a giant Martian lake.

Of course, there was always the chance that *Spirit* would not find evidence of past water at Gusev. Even if a lake had been there in the past, it was possible that the rocks and dirt formed in the lake were now buried beneath many newer lay-

Satellites Orbiting Mars

Mars Global Surveyor (*MGS*). Launched in 1996, the *Mars Global Surveyor* was an enormous success and returned 240,000 images of Mars, more than any previous mission. Its Thermal Emission Spectrometer (TES) analyzed heat given off from Mars's surface. That analysis revealed the presence of the mineral hematite in many of the rocks. (On Earth, hematite typically forms in standing water.) In addition, cameras onboard the *MGS* found an area of waving, curved ridges which, according to the scientists, appear to have been formed as flowing water created an ancient river delta. The *MGS* sent its last transmission to Earth on November 2, 2006. Scientists believe a faulty solar array, which caused the batteries to fail, may be responsible for the spacecraft's loss of communication to Earth.

Mars Odyssey. Launched in 2001, *Mars Odyssey* provides high-resolution images of the entire surface of Mars. These pictures have improved scientific understanding of the planet's climate and geologic history and aid in the search for water and life-sustaining environments. *Mars Odyssey* has discovered evidence of underground Martian ice, and what appears to be the entrances to seven caves near the planet's equator, high on a volcano called Arisia Mons.

Mars Express. Launched by the European Space Agency in 2003, this was Europe's first mission to another planet. The mission included a landing vehicle, *Beagle 2,* but it was lost upon arrival at Mars. *Mars Express* continues to orbit and has produced photographic evidence of dust-covered plates on what appears to be a frozen sea near Mars's equator. Scientists hypothesize that the dust preserved the ice, preventing it from evaporating into the Martian atmosphere. This area is a target for future exploration.

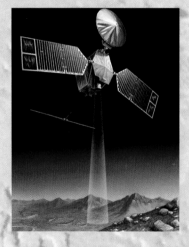

Mars Reconnaissance Orbiter (*MRO*). Launched in 2005, this orbiter is looking for minerals that form in water over a long period of time. It will try to answer the question of whether Mars has ever had water long enough to provide a habitat for life. It will also determine if the underground ice discovered by the *Mars Odyssey* orbiter is shallow or deep. The *MRO* will provide communication links for future spacecraft traveling to Mars.

* Images are artists' conceptions. *NASA/JPL*

ers of dirt and rocks that formed after the lake dried up. There was no way to know what kinds of rock were there until *Spirit* examined them.

Instead of heading for a crater, *Opportunity* was going to land at a smooth plain called Meridiani Planum, halfway around Mars. One of the satellites orbiting Mars at the time, the *Mars Global Surveyor (MGS)*, had an instrument onboard that could detect the presence of minerals in rocks. The *MGS* had sent information back to Earth indicating that Meridiani Planum was rich in a mineral called hematite. On Earth, hematite almost always forms in liquid water. However, hematite can form in hot lava, too. Scientists hoped *Opportunity* would be able to tell which kind of hematite was at Meridiani Planum.

Scientists were not looking for life at Gusev Crater or Meridiani Planum. Instead, they were looking for places where evidence of *past* life might have been preserved. John Grant was the Landing Site Science Coordinator for this mission. In a press release on January 22, 2004, two days before *Opportunity* was scheduled to land at Meridiani Planum, he said, "There's so much we don't know about Mars. But I really think we're going to come out of this mission with a better understanding of what Mars has been like over time, and where we might go for our next step."

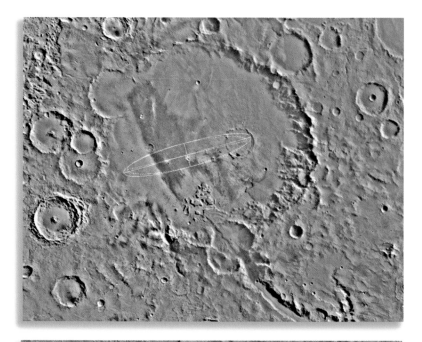

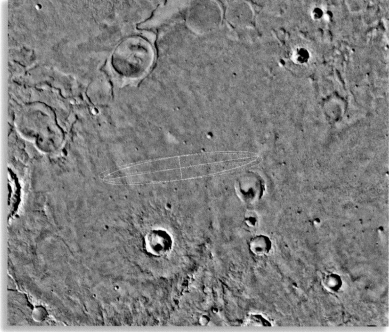

TOP: A Viking image of Gusev Crater, landing site for *Spirit*. *NASA/JPL*

BOTTOM: A Viking image of Meridiani Planum, landing site for *Opportunity*. *NASA/JPL*

6. LAUNCHES AND LANDINGS

The next step for the *MER* mission was getting *to* Mars, which has never been easy. Humans have been trying to send missions to Mars since 1960. The United States had its first success with *Mariner 4* in 1964, but well over half of the 39 attempts have failed, for one reason or another. Sending a mission to Mars is a difficult task, full of potential failures, and everyone's fingers were crossed as "launch day" for *Spirit* and *Opportunity* approached.

NASA can't send a mission to Mars anytime the agency feels like it. There are only a few weeks every two years or so when Mars is relatively close to the Earth, during which spacecraft can be launched toward the Red Planet. These weeks are called the mission's "launch window." Launch windows are different for every space mission and are decided by, among other things, the spacecraft's destination in relation to Earth's position. If the flight is headed to another planet, then the launch window is determined in part by where that planet is in its orbit around the Sun.

As the planets in our solar system revolve in their orbits, at certain times they come closer to the Sun and the other planets

Mars (at top of photograph) in the night sky over Boston on August 27, 2003. *Richard Feinberg/Sky and Telescope Magazine*

in the solar system, and at other times they move farther away from them. On August 27, 2003, Mars orbited closer to Earth than it had in 60,000 years. The last time it came this close, Neanderthals were roaming the Earth! And Mars won't come so close to Earth again until August 28, 2287.

NASA didn't need to launch the rovers toward Mars exactly on August 27, but it did want to set the launch windows some-time during the summer of 2003. Although Mars was closer in

An artist's rendition of Mars's previous close approach to Earth, approximately 60,000 years ago. *NASA/JPL*

2003 than it had been in tens of thousands of years, it comes close enough to Earth for a launch every 26 months. As they planned for this mission, everyone knew if the rovers failed to launch in the summer of 2003, NASA could try again in two years. But nobody wanted to wait that long.

After careful calculations, NASA set the launch window for *Spirit* from June 8 to June 24, 2003. *Opportunity*'s launch window would begin on June 25, 2003, and last until July 15.

Dates are not the only consideration when planning a launch—the time of day is important as well. The times for a launch are dependent on, among other things, where Earth and the planets are in their rotations. When a spacecraft leaves Earth to travel to Mars, it must be headed in a very specific direction. Since Earth is constantly rotating, the launch site is aligned in the proper direction only twice each day—and then only for an instant. If the spacecraft doesn't launch at *precisely* the correct time, once it is in flight it can correct for the error by using its propulsion system to make small adjustments. But fuel is limited on a spacecraft, so only a minor adjustment can be worked into the launch times. It is important that the vehicles launch exactly on schedule. *Spirit* launched on June 10 at precisely 1:58:47, not quite two o'clock in the afternoon. *Opportunity* launched a few weeks later, on July 7 at 11:18:15 at night.

Not only is the precise timing of a launch important, there also has to be enough energy to lift the spacecraft off the launch pad and send it on its way. A bird, a plane, anything that flies uses energy to leave the surface of the Earth. But birds and planes are still subject to the laws of gravity. They cannot escape Earth's pull. Around 62 miles from Earth's surface, our planet's atmosphere thins to the point that it disappears. Technically, this is where space begins. (By comparison, a commercial airliner flies about 7.5 miles above Earth's surface on a long-distance flight.)

In order to escape Earth's gravity and arrive in space, an object has to travel at least 25,000 miles per hour. That figure—25,000 mph—is called Earth's "escape velocity." Every planet has an escape velocity. It varies, depending on the amount of gravity of the planet. Mars is smaller than Earth and therefore it has less gravity. Its escape velocity is only 11,000 mph.

A Delta II rocket launches *Spirit* toward Mars. As Steve Squyres wrote in his book, *Roving Mars,* "None of us would ever see her again, with our own eyes, and that made me surprisingly sad. It was hard to let go."
NASA/Kennedy Space Center

Opportunity lifts off from Launch Complex 17-B at Cape Canaveral. *NASA/Kennedy Space Center*

In order to get to Mars, *Spirit* and *Opportunity* would have to be blasted away from Earth's gravity. Each rover, within its protective shell and packed inside its cruise stage, was perched on top of a mighty Delta II rocket, which is called the "launch vehicle." A launch vehicle is chosen based on the weight it has to launch into space. At liftoff, the Delta II rockets and the spacecraft they carried each weighed 628,820 pounds. It took 200,000 pounds of force, or thrust, to put that much weight into orbit. According to NASA, that amount of thrust is the same as if the water from 2,000 fire hoses was compressed into one single hose 4.7 feet in diameter!

When *Spirit* launched, Mars was 64 million miles away, but because the planets are constantly moving in their orbits, by landing day, seven months later, Mars was about 105.7 million miles away from Earth. When *Opportunity* launched on July 7, 2003, Mars had actually moved a little closer to Earth—it was 48 million miles away. Nevertheless, when *Opportunity* landed, the Earth-Mars distance had expanded to 123.5 million miles.

Launches are dangerous. A lot can go wrong with a rocket that is hurling a payload into space at over 25,000 mph. And a lot can go wrong with landings, too. Many things had to happen exactly right, or the rovers might not survive their descent. NASA planned for each rover to approach Mars tucked inside the cruise stage of its spacecraft. (The cruise stage is the section of the spacecraft that is specially equipped with heaters and insulation to protect the rovers, and electronics to keep the craft on course for Mars and in communication with Earth.) As the spacecraft approached Mars, it would be traveling at about 23,125 miles per hour. Then, as it approached the top of Mars's atmosphere, it was to slow down to 12,000 mph, while the cruise stage was jettisoned, or left behind.

1. Rocket ascends into space.

2. Nose cone separates.

4. Descent to the surface.

5. Landing on the surface.

3. Fiery entry into Martian atmosphere.

6. Rover emerging..

Once the cruise stage was gone, the protective shell that contained the lander and the rover would be exposed to the atmosphere of Mars. Engineers knew that there would be friction as the protective shell fell through the Martian atmosphere, and that the shell would heat up to 2,600 degrees F, but the rover would be protected. The friction would also slow the lander down—to about 960 mph. Then, two minutes before touchdown, if all went as planned, parachutes would open. Twenty seconds later, the bottom half of the protective shell would drop away, exposing the lander and its precious cargo. The lander would still be attached to the top part of the shell by a straplike device called a tether. When the package was 49 feet from the Martian surface, the tether would automatically be cut. Airbags would open up, turning the lander—and its rover—into a giant bouncing ball. When it finally bounced to a stop, motors would pull the airbags away from the lander, the lander would open, and *Spirit* would take its first look at its new Martian home. Then a few weeks later, *Opportunity* would do the same. If all went well.

Artists' conceptions of the launch and landing sequence. *NASA/JPL*

7. DOING SCIENCE

Fortunately, all did go well. With both rovers safely on Mars, the scientists were ready to go to work.

Spirit arrived on Mars on January 3, 2004. When it sent its first pictures back to Earth, everyone was astonished at what they saw. For the first time, Mars could be seen almost as clearly as if the viewer was right there on the planet. But after the excitement of seeing the pictures began to fade, disappointment took its place. As *Spirit* examined the rocks around its landing site at Gusev Crater, little evidence was found that any of them had formed in water. Steve Squyres said, "The spot where we've touched down is not exactly a geologically thrilling locale." The landing site seemed to be covered with lava.

In the spring of 2004, scientists ordered *Spirit* to move on and head toward a series of hills in the distance. The Mars science team named them the "Columbia Hills," after the fallen space shuttle and its crew. (On February 1, 2003, the space shuttle *Columbia* exploded upon reentry into Earth's atmosphere. All seven members of the crew—Rick Husband, William McCool, Michael Anderson, Ilan Ramon, Kalpana

Spirit's first view of Gusev Crater. *NASA/JPL/Cornell*

Columbia Hills Complex

Anderson Hill
95.2° Azimuth
3.1 Kilometers

Brown Hill
97.4° Azimuth
2.9 Kilometers

Chawla Hill
100.8° Azimuth
3.0 Kilometers

Clark Hill
106.1° Azimuth
3.0 Kilometers

Husband Hill
113.9° Azimuth
3.1 Kilometers

Mc Cool Hill
125.1° Azimuth
4.2 Kilometers

Ramon Hill
129.7° Azimuth
4.4 Kilometers

Chawla, David Brown, and Laurel Clark—were killed.) Since the *Columbia* mission carried a payload of scientific experiments, it seemed particularly appropriate that the Mars science team named individual peaks of the Columbia Hills after these astronauts.

Meanwhile, *Opportunity* had landed on Meridiani Planum. The name *Opportunity* turned out to be a good fit for this rover, because right from the beginning of this mission it seemed to get lots of opportunities to find evidence of water on Mars. In

The distant peaks of Columbia Hills, named for fallen astronauts. *NASA/JPL*

the first place, in a stroke of luck that Steve Squyres compared to throwing an object from New York City to Los Angeles and having it hit within a half inch of its target, *Opportunity* landed inside a small crater, right next to an exposed area of bedrock. Usually, bedrock is buried beneath layers of soil, sand, or gravel; geologists on Earth often have to dig for it. Finding exposed bedrock on Mars was a wonderful break. And other exciting news was yet to come.

After months of careful exploration, using all of the tools onboard *Opportunity*, the reward for the many years of planning and work finally came. *Opportunity* found what the scientists were looking for. There was mineral evidence that proved water had once drenched and flowed over the rover's landing site. "NASA's *Opportunity* rover has demonstrated some rocks on Mars probably formed as deposits at the bottom of a body of gently flowing saltwater," said Steve Squyres. "We think *Opportunity* is parked on what was once the shoreline of a salty sea on Mars." There had been water on Mars—and not just at the poles!

Opportunity's first view of Meridiani Planum. Note the collapsed airbag in front of the rover. *NASA/JPL/Cornell*

Mars landscape showing exposed bedrock. *NASA/JPL*

This was the kind of news everyone had been hoping to get: In its ancient past, Mars had once had a habitable climate where life could exist. But as Steve Squyres cautiously added, "It doesn't mean life was there, but this was a habitable place." Back at Gusev Crater, the story had changed, too.

Any good scientist has to believe what the evidence tells him. Members of the MER science team had thought that Gusev Crater was once a large Martian lake, but by 2006 *Spirit* had still not found clues about any water having been there. As Steve Squyres said, "We have absolutely seen no evidence for surface water." The rocks of Columbia Hills, however, told a different story. They contained hematite and other minerals that form in the presence of water. It appeared that long ago there was also water in the Columbia Hills. But the most exciting discovery for *Spirit* was still ahead.

In May 2007 *Spirit* found a patch of nearly pure silica, which on Earth is used as the main ingredient in window glass. Silica is produced in one of two kinds of environments—either a hot spring or an acidic steam vent called a fumarole. In a NASA press release dated December 10, 2007, Steve Squyres

Space Junk

Have you ever wondered what happens to all the spaceships and satellites that are launched into space? Most do not return to Earth. Those that land on planets, such as the rover *Sojourner* and the MER rovers, remain there indefinitely after they stop functioning. Satellites, too, often remain in orbit around Earth or other planets long after their jobs are done, although some are taken down if it looks as though their orbits are in danger of disintegrating. Smaller debris from spacecraft—both manned and unmanned—frequently falls toward Earth and is destroyed as it descends through the heat of Earth's atmosphere. Other debris, however, remains as a blanket of space junk in orbit around Earth or other planets. One NASA estimate says there are over 9,000 pieces of space junk—from astronaut Ed White's lost glove, to bolts and screws dropped during spacewalks, to pieces from spent rockets and broken satellites—all still in orbit.

stated, "Whichever of those conditions produced it, this concentration of silica is probably the most significant discovery by *Spirit* for revealing a habitable niche that existed on Mars in the past." Here was more evidence that Earth and Mars—at some time long ago—were similar planets. On Earth, microbial life flourishes in hot springs and fumaroles. Mars had either hot springs or fumaroles—perhaps both. The existence of those features raises the question of whether those environments could have supported microbial life on Mars, too.

Spirit discovered silica on Mars. Such soil had never been found on Mars before.
Mars Exploration Rover Mission/Cornell/JPL/NASA

You are here

The first picture of Earth taken from the surface of a planet beyond the Moon. *NASA/JPL/Cornell/Texas A&M*

This 180-million-year-old meteorite, discovered in Antarctica, is almost certainly from Mars. It contains a small amount of gas that is chemically identical to the Martian atmosphere. *NASA Johnson Space Center/LPI*

Not only have *Spirit* and *Opportunity* found what they were looking for, they have also lasted far longer than anyone working on this mission dreamed they would. Eventually, they will quit working, but science will be studying the information they provided for years to come. Most scientists believe that Mars was once more like Earth than it is today. No one knows exactly what happened to make it change. The majority of scientists believe that water was once there, but right now no one understands what made it disappear—or if the same thing could happen on Earth. There are some scientists who believe that they have already discovered fossilized microbial life in a Martian meteorite that hit Earth. Other scientists disagree with

Mars Time

A day on Earth lasts for 24 hours, but a Mars day, or sol, lasts for 24 hours, 39 minutes, and 35 seconds—the length of time it takes Mars to rotate once on its axis. In order to adjust their bodies to the work schedule of the rovers, scientists had to work on Mars time. To help with the adjustment, they hung blackout curtains over the windows in their building at JPL, and they had special clocks and watches made that marked off the hours in Mars time.

Everyone expected the mission would only last for 90 days, and then it would be over. But *Spirit* and *Opportunity* continued to work for years! As of May 2008, the rovers were still working on Mars. They had been on the planet for three Earth years, which is more than 12 times the duration of their original 90-day mission. Long before this, the engineers and scientists were able to return to living their lives by Earth time. On October 15, 2007, NASA announced that the rovers' mission will be extended for a fifth time, through 2009, provided they continue to operate well.

A master watchmaker, Garo Anserlian, made this watch face for telling time on Mars. His first Mars watch accurately told Martian time within ten seconds. *NASA/JPL*

that finding. But so far, no one has yet discovered past or present microbial life on Mars. Future missions will try to answer such questions. However, whether life, even a microbe so tiny it can only be seen with a microscope, has ever lived on Mars or not, NASA is examining the possibilities that one day human beings will be able to live there.

8. IMAGINE THE FUTURE

In September 1962, in a speech delivered at Rice University in Houston, Texas, President John F. Kennedy uttered these words: "We choose to go to the Moon. We choose to go to the Moon in this decade and do the other things, not because they are easy but because they hard." On July 20, 1969—almost at the end of that decade—Neil Armstrong took humanity's first steps on the moon. It wasn't easy to get there, but we did it.

In January 2004, President George W. Bush declared another ambitious plan. The United States would send more human missions to the Moon—and to Mars. That announcement came 42 years after President Kennedy's statement. The new plan is called the NASA Vision for Space Exploration, and like the Apollo Project that sent humans to the Moon, a human mission to Mars will not be easy to achieve. It will be very difficult. But like Apollo, it too can be done—if certain problems are overcome.

The trip to Mars is a long one. A one-way flight could take seven months, and that is a long time for anyone—even a well-trained astronaut—to be confined inside a small spaceship. However, it might be possible to improve upon this time with

Mars, showing its southern polar ice cap. *NASA/JPL*

Earth or Mars? Which image is which?
(*Answer:* Earth is on the left.)
Earth image: Filipe Alves
Mars image: MER mission/JPL/NASA

newer, more powerful rockets, which would travel through space faster.

Although the astronauts could carry food for their journey with them, once they arrived on Mars, getting enough food would be a problem. Because Earth and Mars come into good alignment for space travel once every two years, a human mission to Mars would probably last for three years, counting the time it takes to make the trip each way. Supply ships could not come and go on a regular basis. Once on the planet, astronauts would have to grow their own crops in special greenhouses that would protect the plants from the Sun's radiation. And, of course, living things need water. This is why finding evidence of water on Mars—even if it's in the form of ice—is so important for any future colonization missions.

Spirit and *Opportunity* looked for evidence of past water on Mars. The *Phoenix* Mars spacecraft, launched on August 4, 2007, landed near Mars's north pole on May 25, 2008. A back-hoe onboard *Phoenix* will dig into Mars's polar ice, which lies below a thin layer of soil. The soil and water ice will be brought to the lander's platform, where instruments will per-

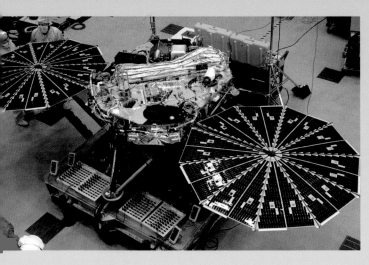

Phoenix Mars Lander with solar arrays open. In order to capture energy from the Sun, the solar arrays will remain open on Mars.
NASA/JPL/UA/Lockheed Martin

An artist's conception of a crew drilling on Mars.
NASA/JPL

form scientific analysis for life. Water ice is important for future missions, too, because it can be melted into water, then purified and used for drinking, bathing, and watering the crops in the greenhouse.

Water can also be used to make fuel. Water is made up of two elements—hydrogen and oxygen—and these elements can be distilled, or separated out. Spaceship fuel contains both hydrogen and oxygen. Hydrogen provides the fire in some of the liquid-fuel engines, and oxygen is what keeps those fires burning. Scientists are thinking about ways to use the molecules of hydrogen and oxygen to create the kind of fuel needed to send the spaceship on a return journey to Earth.

Mars's atmosphere is made up of carbon dioxide and a few other elements, including a trace of oxygen. Humans need oxygen to breathe, and once again water could help. Not only would the oxygen distilled out of Martian water be useful in making fuel, but, scientists theorize, it could also be used to create a breathable atmosphere for human habitats, as well as the plants' greenhouse.

All of these plans sound more like science fiction than real science, yet NASA, in cooperation with the SETI (Search for Extraterrestrial Intelligence) Institute and the Mars Institute, is already doing research on how human beings could live on Mars. That research is being conducted at places on Earth that are similar to Mars in some ways.

Astronaut Donald R. Pettit spent 161 days conducting various scientific experiments onboard the International Space Station, the space habitat orbiting Earth where astronauts live for extended periods of time. Speaking at Rice University on October 26, 2007, Dr. Pettit said, "You don't train for spaceflight by doing spaceflight"—meaning, you train not in space but on Earth, in conditions resembling as closely as possible the conditions of space. Before going aboard the space station, Dr. Pettit trained on Earth for his mission by simulating—or mimicking—what life in space would be like. Others are now beginning to do the same kinds of earthly simulations of life on Mars.

This type of training and experimentation is taking place at two important sites on Earth. The Haughton-Mars Project on Devon Island in the Canadian Arctic simulates Martian life in a cold, rocky, windswept, barren part of the world. Another important location is in the Utah desert, near Hanksville,

LEFT: The Mars Desert Research Station in Utah.
The Mars Society

BELOW: A researcher working at the Haughton-Mars research station in the Arctic. The greenhouse for growing food is in the background.
CSA ASC/ The Mars Institute/NASA/SETI

On May 19, 2005, *Spirit* used its panoramic camera to capture this sunset over Gusev Crater. Future colonists on Mars may one day marvel at a similar sight. *NASA/JPL/Texas A & M/Cornell*

Utah. In both places, scientists live and work as if they were living and working on Mars. They wear spacesuits, they live in habitats, and they grow food in greenhouses. They perform research on the rocks and dirt that surround them, and they monitor how they get along with each other in such a controlled environment. All of this information—and much more—will be essential as NASA plans for real missions to the Red Planet. In addition to scientists, students 18 years old and above may apply to work in one of these habitats for a period of weeks. Many aspiring astronauts apply for the program.

Traveling to Mars, living in an alien world in a cramped habitat, wearing a spacesuit any time you leave the habitat, harvesting water or ice where you find it, growing food in a greenhouse, learning to walk without the pull of Earth's gravity —none of it will be easy. But it wasn't easy for the first humans to leave Africa and move out across the plains of Asia and Europe. It wasn't easy for Ferdinand Magellan to circumnavigate the Earth. And it wasn't easy for Neil Armstrong to become the first person to step on the surface of the moon. However, human beings are adventurous creatures, and exploring space is one of the most exciting—and most challenging—adventures of all. This adventure will continue, not because it is easy, but because it is human nature to explore.

An artist's conception of the *Phoenix* making a powered landing on Mars. *NASA/JPL*

The *Mars Science Laboratory* will collect rock and soil samples to test them for signs of life. (Artist's conception.) *NASA/JPL*

Artist's conception of future scout missions, which may use balloons and/or airplanes. *NASA/JPL*

This type of ascent vehicle will send Martian soil samples back to Earth for study and analysis. (Artist's conception.) *NASA/JPL*

AFTERWORD: Future Missions to Mars

Science always builds on the discoveries of the past, and it may be several more years before a manned mission to Mars is ready to be launched. However, *Spirit* and *Opportunity* have provided valuable information about Mars that NASA will use as it plans future unmanned missions to the Red Planet. Right now, these are the missions that are planned for the next several years:

PHOENIX MARS MISSION
Launch: August 2007
Arrival on Mars: May 2008
On May 25, 2008, as this book went to press, the Phoenix spacecraft landed sucessfully on the frozen arctic plains of Mars. Its instruments will claw down into the ice and dirt and analyze both for any signs of life, or for the ingredients that make up life.

MARS SCIENCE LABORATORY
Launch: Fall 2009
Arrival on Mars: October 2010
The *Mars Science Laboratory* is another rover that will collect Martian soil and analyze it for conditions that could have supported microbial life.

MARS SAMPLE RETURN
Beginning around 2020, this most complicated mission would collect samples of Martian soil and return them to Earth, where they could be studied in laboratories.

ASTROBIOLOGY FIELD LABORATORY
This future mission would conduct a search for life on Mars. It would use the information gathered by the 2009 *Mars Science Laboratory* to identify any chemical building blocks for life, as we know it, that might be present on Mars.

Glossary

asteroid: a small celestial body in orbit around the Sun.

astronaut: a person trained to travel into space.

astronomer: a scientist who studies the motion, size, and composition of celestial bodies.

atom: the smallest possible unit, or part, of any chemical element.

axis: an imaginary line through an object like a planet around which the object revolves.

canal: a constructed waterway.

canyon: a narrow valley with steep cliffs on each side.

carbon dioxide: a gas made up of carbon and oxygen.

celestial body: a natural object, such as a star or planet, in space.

channel: a narrow body of water that connects two other bodies of water.

comet: an object in orbit around the Sun thought to be made of dust and gas, with a long vaporous tail when within a certain distance of the Sun.

concave: having an inward curve, like the inside of a bowl.

convex: having an outward curve, like the surface of a ball.

crater: a bowl-shaped depression on the surface of a moon or planet.

cruise stage: the section of a spacecraft that houses instruments and equipment for a journey.

debris: scattered pieces of an object that has been destroyed.

earth orbit: the path of an object around the Earth.

energy: the force it takes to make something move or change.

engineer: a person trained to use scientific knowledge to solve practical problems, such as building robots, roads, buildings, etc.

ESA: European Space Agency, which is responsible for regulating European space flight.

escape velocity: the speed required to leave the gravitational pull of a planet or moon.

evidence: knowledge or information that is used as a basis for belief.

flyby: a mission that sends a spacecraft close enough to its target to gather information without landing.

fossil: the remains of a once-living organism embedded in the Earth's crust.

fumarole: an opening in the Earth's surface that emits gas and/or steam, usually found near volcanic areas.

geologist: a person who studies the origin, structure, and history of the Earth and other planets.

gravity: the force of attraction exerted by a celestial body, such as Earth.

greenhouse: a structure that protects growing plants from a harsh environment.

habitat: a structure with a controlled environment that provides shelter from the environment.

hematite: an iron mineral that usually forms in water.

hydrogen: a colorless, odorless gas that is the lightest and most abundant element in the universe.

hypothesis: a proposed scientific explanation based on observation.

International Space Station: a habitat in low earth orbit that houses an international crew of astronauts.

JPL: the Jet Propulsion Laboratory, a division of NASA.

landers: vehicles designed to land and remain on the surface of planets.

launch: to send something into space.

launch vehicle: the rocket used to launch a spacecraft or satellite into space.

launch window: specific period of time during which a spacecraft may be launched.

lava: hot melted rock that erupts from a volcano; also that same rock once it has cooled and solidified.

magnet: an object surrounded by a magnetic field that can pull iron toward itself.

meteorite: a stony or metallic object that has fallen to the Earth's surface from outer space.

microbial life: life so small it can be seen only with a microscope.

mineral: a substance formed in the earth that was never animal or vegetable.

molecule: the smallest part of a substance that still has all the properties of that substance; a molecule is made of one or more atoms.

NASA: U.S. government agency responsible for regulating American spaceflight.

Neanderthals: an ancient human species who lived approximately 250,000 to 30,000 years ago.

optical illusion: a false or deceptive visual impression.

orbit: the path a celestial body or object takes as it revolves around another.

oxygen: a gas, with no color or smell, that all animals need for life.

payload: passengers, crew, instruments, or equipment carried by a spacecraft.

rocket, or **rocket engine:** the energy source for sending spacecraft into space.

rotation: a single complete turn on an axis.

rover: robotic vehicle used to explore terrain of a planet or moon and perform scientific experiments.

satellite: a celestial body, like a moon, that orbits a planet, or a manmade object launched to orbit a planet or other celestial body.

silica: a mineral found in sand, rock, and quartz.

sol: a Martian day, 24 hours, 39 minutes, and 35 seconds long.

solar system: a star and the collection of solar bodies that orbit it.

space: the part of the universe beyond Earth's atmosphere.

spacecraft: a vehicle that is launched into space.

space shuttle: spacecraft that flies in low Earth orbit.

spectrum: light broken into its component colors, or wavelengths (as seen in a rainbow).

spectrometer: an instrument that analyzes light by breaking it into its wavelengths, or spectrum.

telescope: an instrument that uses lenses, mirrors, and sometimes cameras to make distant objects appear larger and closer.

volcano: a mountain made from melted rock that builds up around a fumarole.

For Further Exploration

AUTHOR'S NOTE AND BIBLIOGRAPHY

This book began on August 27, 2003, the day of Mars's closest approach to Earth in 60,000 years. I was at the Rice Observatory that evening, and I had the privilege of viewing Mars through the university's 16-inch Meade telescope. It was an amazing sight, and from that evening on, I had Mars on my mind. I began to read more about the planet, and in 2004 I received an invitation to attend a lecture at the University of Houston, Clear Lake given by Dr. Agustin Chicarro, Project Scientist, Mars Express, and Dr. Steven Squyres, Principal Investigator, Mars Exploration Rover Mission. The men lectured on March 16, 2004, and their topic was "Early Results from the Mars Missions." Their lecture was so exciting, I could barely keep still in my seat! Then, on September 14, 2004, I attended the annual William F. Marlar Lecture at Rice University. Dr. Geoffrey W. Marcy, Professor of Astronomy at the University of California, Berkeley was the speaker, and his topic was "Planets, Yellowstone, and the Prospects for Life in the Universe." In general, he talked about the fact that scientists have found microbial life in very unlikely places here on Earth, such as the rocks, geysers, and hot springs of Yellowstone National Park, hypothesizing on the possibility that similar life could exist on other planets in our solar system. I began to wonder if the rovers would find evidence of this type of life on Mars, either in its past or even the present. The idea for *Mars and the Search for Life* began to take shape. Later in the research process, on October 26, 2007, I attended a lecture sponsored by the James A. Baker III Institute for Public Policy at Rice University. That lecture was delivered by Dr. Donald R. Pettit, NASA astronaut, who spoke on "The Antarctic Search for Meteorites, Some Observations Relevant to Long-Duration Space Flights." All of these lectures provided invaluable information for this book.

The Jet Propulsion Laboratory in Pasadena, California, in conjunction with the California Institute of Technology, is the leading center for robotic exploration of the solar system. Since the rovers' scientific discoveries were taking place in "real time," I read all the information released by JPL as soon as it became available. Those press releases, along with much more information about the MER mission are available at http://marsrovers.jpl.nasa.gov.

Cornell University also maintains a website for the Athena program, and it contains information I used as well. It is located at http://athena.cornell.edu.

I also consulted the following scripts, books, and magazines as I worked on the text:

Couper, Heather, and Nigel Henbest. *How the Universe Works*. Pleasantville, N.Y.: Readers Digest Books, 1994.

Curtis, Anthony R. (ed.) *Space Almanac,* 2nd ed. Houston: Gulf Publishing, 1992.

Hartmann, William K. *A Traveler's Guide to Mars*. New York: Workman Publishing, 2003.

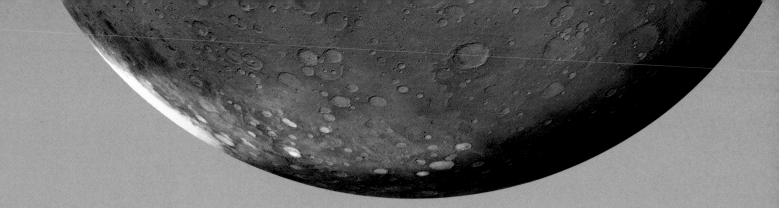

Koch, Howard. "The War of the Worlds" script for Mercury Theater on the Air, ca. 1940.

Morton, Oliver. "Mars: Is There Life in the Ancient Ice?" *National Geographic*. January 2004, pages 5–30.

Lowell, Percival. *Mars*. Whitefish, Mont.: Kessinger Publishing, 2004. (Originally published by Houghton Mifflin and Company, 1895.)

Squyres, Steve. *Roving Mars*. New York: Hyperion, 2005.

Wells, H. G. *The War of the Worlds* (Tor Classics) New York: Tom Doherty Associates, 1993. (Originally published by Heinemann Publishers, 1898.)

You may also find the following sources to be of interest.

BOOKS

Croswell, Ken. *Ten Worlds: Everything That Orbits the Sun*. Honesdale, Pa.: Boyds Mills, 2006.

Florian, Douglas. *Comets, Stars, the Moon, and Mars: Space Poems and Paintings*. Orlando, Fla.: Harcourt Children's Books, 2007.

Getz, David. *Life on Mars*. New York: Henry Holt and Co., 2004.

Hakim, Joy. *The Story of Science: Aristotle Leads the Way*. Washington, D.C.: Smithsonian Books, 2004.

Krull, Kathleen. *The Night the Martians Landed: Just the Facts (Plus the Rumors) About Invaders from Mars*. New York: HarperCollins, 2003.

Leedy, Loren, and Andrew Schuerger. *Messages from Mars*. New York: Holiday House, 2006.

Malone, Robert. *Ultimate Robot*. New York: DK Publishing, 2004.

Miller, Ron. *Satellites*. Minneapolis, Minn.: Twenty-First Century Books, 2007.

Ride, Sally, and Tam O'Shaughnessy. *The Mystery of Mars*. New York: Crown Books for Young Readers, 1999.

Skurzynski, Gloria. *Are We Alone? Scientists Search for Life in Space*. Washington, D.C.: National Geographic Children's Books, 2004.

Taschek, Karen. *Death Stars, Weird Galaxies, and a Quasar-Spangled Universe: The Discoveries of the Very Large Array Telescope*. Albuquerque, N. Mex.: Univ. of New Mexico Press, 2006.

Ward, David J. *Exploring Mars*. Minneapolis, Minn.: Lerner, 2006.

WEBSITES

Athena Mars Exploration Rovers
http://www.athena.cornell.edu

Mars Exploration
http://mars.jpl.nasa.gov

The Mars Society
http://www.marssociety.org/portal

ASU Mars Education Program
http://marsed.asu.edu

Index

Note: Page numbers in **bold** type refer to illustrations.